NETWORKS

SAND
SCULPTURES

John McInnes, *Senior Author*
Clayton Graves
Christine McClymont

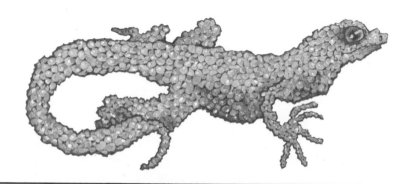

NELSON CANADA

© Nelson Canada,
A Division of International Thomson Limited, 1988

Published in 1988 by
Nelson Canada,
A Division of International Thomson Limited
1120 Birchmount Road
Scarborough, Ontario
M1K 5G4

ISBN 0-17-602506-5

Canadian Cataloguing in Publication Data
Main entry under title:

Sand sculptures

(Networks)
ISBN 0-17-602506-5

1. Readers (Primary).   I. McInnes, John, 1927-
II. Graves, Clayton.   III. McClymont, Christine.
IV. Series: Networks (Toronto, Ont.).

PE1119.S36 1987   428.6   C87-094285-9

Printed and bound in Canada

Contents

The Circle of Friends

...*is always open*.

Stevie

by John Steptoe

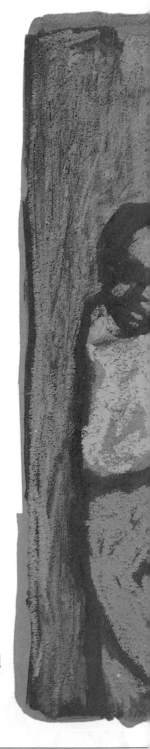

One day my momma told me, "You know you're gonna have a little friend come stay with you."

And I said, "Who is it?"

And she said, "You know my friend Mrs. Mack? Well, she has to work all week and I'm gonna keep her little boy."

I asked, "For how long?"

She said, "He'll stay all week and his mother will come pick him up on Saturdays."

The next day the doorbell rang. It was a lady and a kid. He was smaller than me. I ran to my mother. "Is that them?"

They went in the kitchen but I stayed out in the hall to listen.

The little boy's name was Steven but his mother kept calling him Stevie. My name is Robert but my momma don't call me Robertie.

And so Steve moved in, with his old crybaby self. He always had to have his way. And he was greedy too. Everything he sees he wants. "Could I have somma that? Gimme this." Man!

Since he was littler than me, while I went to school he used to stay home and play with my toys. I wished his mother would bring somma *his* toys over here to break up.

I used to get so mad at my mother when I came home after school. "Momma, can't you watch him and tell him to leave my stuff alone?"

Then he used to like to get up on my bed to look out the window and leave his dirty footprints all over my bed. And my momma never said nothin' to him.

And on Saturdays when his mother comes to pick him up, he always tries to act cute just cause his mother is there. He picked up my airplane and I told him not to bother it. He thought I wouldn't say nothin' to him in front of his mother.

I could never go anywhere without my mother sayin' "Take Stevie with you now."

"But why I gotta take him everywhere I go?" I'd say.

"Now if you were stayin' with someone you wouldn't want them to treat you mean," my mother told me. "Why don't you and Stevie try to play nice?"

Yeah, but I always been nice to him with his old spoiled self. He's always gotta have his way anyway.

I had to take him out to play with me and my friends.

"Is that your brother, Bobby?" they'd ask me.

"No."

"Is that your cousin?"

"No! He's just my friend and he's stayin' at my house and my mother made me bring him."

"Ha, ha. You gotta baby-sit! Bobby the baby-sitter!"

"Aw, be quiet. Come on, Steve. See! Why you gotta make all my friends laugh for?"

"Ha, ha. Bobby the baby-sitter," my friends said.

"Hey, come on, y'all, let's go play in the park. You comin', Bobby?" one of my friends said.

"Naw, my momma said he can't go in the park cause the last time he went he fell and hurt his knee, with his old stupid self."

And then they left.

"You see? You see! I can't even play with my friends. Man! Come on."

"I'm sorry, Robert. You don't like me, Robert? I'm sorry," Stevie said.

"Aw, be quiet. That's okay," I told him.

One time when my daddy was havin' company I was just sittin' behind the couch just listenin' to them talk. And I wasn't makin' no noise. They didn't even know I was there! Then here comes Stevie with his old loud self. Then when my father heard him, he yelled at *me* and told me to go upstairs.

Sometimes people get on your nerves and they don't mean it or nothin' but they just bother you. Why I gotta put up with him? My momma only had one kid. I used to have a lot of fun before old stupid came to live with us.

One Saturday Steve's mother and father came to my house to pick him up like always. But they said that they were gonna move away and that Stevie wasn't gonna come back anymore.

So then he left. The next mornin' I got up to watch cartoons and I fixed two bowls of corn flakes. Then I just remembered that Stevie wasn't here.

Sometimes we had a lot of fun runnin' in and out of the house. Well, I guess my bed will stay clean from now on. But that wasn't so bad. He couldn't help it cause he was stupid.

I remember the time I ate the last piece of cake in the breadbox and blamed it on him.

I remember when I was doin' my homework I used to try to teach him what I had learned. He could write his name pretty good for his age.

I remember the time we played boogie man and we hid under the covers with Daddy's flashlight.

And that time we was playin' in the park under the bushes and we found these two dead rats and one was brown and one was black.

We used to have some good times together. I think he liked my momma better than his own, cause he used to call his mother "Mother" and he called my momma "Mommy."

Aw, no! I let my corn flakes get soggy thinkin' about him. He was a nice little guy. He was kinda like a little brother.

Little Stevie.

Shouting Doesn't Help

by Sonia Craddock

The yellow school bus pulled to a stop beside a muddy mountain road.

"All out," called the driver to the last two children.

Sonja and Amy jumped off the bus and walked along the road in silence.

It was April and the snow was melting. Little rivers of melting snow ran down the road, and the two girls splashed about in the streams with their rubber boots.

"I'm glad you moved here, Amy," Sonja said after they had walked for a while. "No other children live on this road. I've never had anyone to play with, except at school." She glanced at Amy with a worried look. Maybe Amy wouldn't want to be friends. Maybe Amy wouldn't like her.

Amy tossed back her long black braids and smiled. "I'm glad I moved here too," she said very slowly. "It's so different from the city."

Sonja bit her lip. Maybe Amy would think it was too different. Maybe city kids were different. Maybe Amy only liked city kids. She didn't sound very friendly.

"I think I'm going to be in your grade," Amy said suddenly. "A teacher called Mrs. Banks tested me today and said it would be alright."

Sonja was puzzled. Amy had told her she was ten years old. She should be in grade five, not grade three. And why had Mrs. Banks spent all day testing Amy? It was a mystery.

They arrived at the gate to Sonja's house. Sonja wanted to ask Amy in for some hot chocolate, but she was too shy.

"Goodbye Amy," said Sonja. And then, greatly daring, she called, "Do you want to play later?"

But Amy didn't answer. She just walked round the bend and out of sight.

Tears came to Sonja's eyes. Amy didn't want to be friends. She walked up the driveway and into her house feeling very sad.

The next morning Sonja ran down to the main road and climbed up into the giant maple tree to wait for the school bus. The tree was her private hiding place. She could sit on a broad branch and see all the way up the lake to the town of Nelson, and all the way down the lake to the saw-toothed mountains and the shining white glacier.

Sonja was watching the school bus wind its way down the lake when Amy came in sight, out of breath and running hard.

"It's all right," Sonja shouted down to her. "The bus hasn't come yet. Do you want to climb up here with me?"

But Amy didn't answer her. She didn't even look up into the tree.

She doesn't like me, thought Sonja. She doesn't even want to talk to me.

When the bus came, Sonja slid down the tree and sat by herself at the back of the bus. She didn't look at Amy at all. She pretended to read a book. And when Amy came into the third grade classroom later that morning, Sonja didn't even smile at her.

"Class," said Mrs. Halpern, "We have a new member. Her name is Amy."

"Hi, Amy," everyone except Sonja called out.

"Amy has something she wants to say to you," said Mrs. Halpern.

The children became quiet. They were all wondering what it was that Amy wanted to say.

Amy stood up and faced everybody. "I am deaf," she said in a slow halting voice. "I can't hear. I have to read your lips." And then she sat down very quickly.

There was a buzz all around the class, as everyone talked at once.

"Amy can understand what we say by watching our lips move," Mrs. Halpern said, smiling at Amy. "It helps her if we speak clearly and don't rush our words."

Then the whole class wanted to try and see if they could 'read lips' too. So Mrs. Halpern spoke to them without using her voice. She just moved her lips.

"What did you say? What did you say?" everybody shouted. No one understood her.

"Ask Amy," said Mrs. Halpern.

"She said that it is so warm today that we can go outside for gym," Amy said, and smiled shyly.

Everyone cheered.

"But what if Amy can't see our lips?" Chang called out.

"Well, shouting doesn't help," said Mrs. Halpern. "You must go up to her and touch her on the shoulder. Amy is very good at reading your lips, but she has to be able to see you."

Sonja stared at Amy. Now she understood why Amy hadn't answered her.

At recess she rushed up to Amy, and, standing in front of her, she said, very clearly, "Amy, do you want to be friends?"

Amy gave a big smile. "Yes," she said. "I thought maybe you didn't like me because I couldn't hear."

"I thought you didn't like me because I wasn't from the city," said Sonja.

And they both grinned at one another happily.

Maxie

by Mildred Kantrowitz

Maxie lived in three small rooms on the top floor of an old brownstone house on Orange Street.

She had lived there for many years, and every day was the same for Maxie. Every morning, seven days a week, every morning at exactly seven o'clock, Maxie raised the shades on her three front windows.

Every morning at exactly 7:10, Maxie's large, orange cat jumped up onto the middle windowsill and sprawled there in the morning sun.

At 7:20, if you were watching Maxie's back window, you could see her raise the shade to the very top. Then she uncovered a bird cage. On the perch inside the cage was a yellow canary. He was waiting for his water dish to be filled, and it always was, if you were still watching, at 7:22.

At 8:15 every morning, Maxie's door opened with a tired squeak. Maxie's old, leather slippers made slapping sounds as she walked down the four flights of uncarpeted stairs to the front door. Outside the front door were the bottles of milk in a container. Maxie always tried to hold the door open with her left foot while she reached out to get her milk. But every morning it was just a little too far for her to reach. The door always banged shut and locked behind her.

So, at 8:20 every morning, Maxie rang the bell marked "Superintendent." The superintendent, whose name was Arthur, would open the door for Maxie and let her in with her milk.

Only Maxie and the man at the grocery store knew what she ate for breakfast, but everyone knew she drank tea. At 8:45 every morning, they could hear the whistling of her tea kettle. How Maxie loved that whistle! She loved it so much that she let it sing out for one full minute. Dogs howled, cats whined and babies bawled, but everyone knew that when the whistle stopped, it would be 8:46. And it always was.

The letter carrier knew more about Maxie than anyone else did. He knew that she had a sister in Chicago who sent her a Christmas card every year. He also knew when Maxie planted the flowers in her window boxes because every spring he delivered her seed catalogue. Then a few weeks later he delivered packets of seeds.

Every morning at nine o'clock, Maxie walked down the stairs for the second time in her leather slippers. She went outside and put her small bag of garbage in the pail on the front stoop.

Then she came back in and waited for the letter carrier. She walked slowly past him in the hall, watching him put mail in the slots for the other people who lived in the house.

Maxie climbed the four flights of stairs again, resting at each landing. When she got to the top, Maxie went into her apartment, and the door closed after her with the same tired squeak.

One afternoon at 1:05, just as she did every afternoon at 1:05, Maxie moved the bird cage with the yellow bird in it to the front windows. It was shady and cool there now.

The large, orange cat moved to the back window and sprawled there, soaking up the sun that matched the colour of his fur.

"You're perfectly happy just lying there, day after day," Maxie said to the cat. "All you ever want to do is move from one windowsill to the other and watch the world go by. You don't need anyone, and no one really needs you. But you don't seem to care." Maxie turned away from the window.

"I care," she said sadly. "I'm not a cat. But I might as well be." Maxie felt very tired, and she went to bed.

That was Monday.

On Tuesday morning at seven o'clock, the three shades on Maxie's front windows and the one on her back window remained down. At 7:10, the large orange cat was still asleep at the foot of Maxie's bed. And at 7:30, there were no sweet warbling sounds. That morning no one heard the sounds of Maxie's leather slippers on the stairs. Her tea kettle was filled with empty silence.

At nine o'clock, the letter carrier came with the daily mail. He had a seed catalogue for Maxie and he waited for her to come down the stairs. Since she didn't come and this was most unusual, he decided to deliver the catalogue to her door.

He climbed the four flights of stairs. He knocked and waited. There was no sign of Maxie.

At 9:03, Mr. Turkle who lived on the third floor came hurrying up the stairs. At 9:05, Mr. and Mrs. Moorehouse got there from across the street. At 9:07, Mrs. Trueheart came over from next door. Susie Smith came up at 9:10 with her twin brothers. Five members of the family on the second floor made it up by 9:13. Then came Arthur, the superintendent.

By 9:17, there were seventeen people, three dogs and two cats, all waiting for Maxie to open the door.

And when she didn't they all went in.

They found Maxie in bed.

More people came up the stairs and someone called a doctor. By the time he got there, there were forty-two grown-ups and eleven children in Maxie's small living room.

When the doctor came out of Maxie's bedroom he shook his head sadly. "Maxie isn't really sick," he said. "She's lonely. She doesn't feel loved. She doesn't feel that anyone needs her."

No one said anything for a minute. Then suddenly
Mrs. Trueheart got up and walked right past the doctor
and into the bedroom. "Maxie!" she shouted angrily,
"you let me down. You and that warbling bird let me
down! Every morning I wake up when I hear that bird.
Then it's my job to wake my husband. He has the
morning shift at the corner diner and he's still asleep.
Why, there must be at least seventy-five people at that
diner right now, waiting for their breakfasts. They'll all
have to go to work on empty stomachs—all because of
you and that yellow bird!"

Everyone else crowded into the bedroom. Maxie sat up in bed and listened to what they had to say.

"I couldn't go to school this morning," Susie Smith said. "I missed my bus because I didn't hear your tea kettle whistle."

"The school bus never came this morning," said Mr. Turkle who drove the bus. "I didn't wake up in time. I never heard Sarah Sharpe's footsteps on my ceiling." Sarah Sharpe was a nurse who lived just above Mr. Turkle. There were a lot of people waiting for her right now at the hospital. She always got up when she heard Maxie's door squeak.

Mr. and Mrs. Moorehouse both had very important jobs but they had missed their train that morning. Their alarm clock was Maxie's window shade.

Arthur said he hadn't swept the front steps that morning. He overslept because Maxie didn't ring his bell. He hoped no one would complain.

They all talked about it and decided that there must be about four hundred people who needed Maxie—or who needed someone else who needed Maxie—every morning.

Maxie smiled. She got out of bed and made a pot of tea. In fact, she made five pots of tea. Each time the kettle whistled, dogs howled, cats whined and babies bawled.

Maxie listened and thought about how many people were being touched by these sounds—her sounds. By 9:45 that morning, Maxie had served tea to everybody, and she was so pleased.

Our Good Health

...let's celebrate it!

COME TO THE HEALTH FAIR

Lauren: Would you believe some people have fun when they go to the hospital? That's what our class at Clinton Junior School did this year. We went to the Health Fair at the Hospital for Sick Children.

Robert: It was just like a real fair with coloured balloons, stuffed animals, games to play, a movie, and even cake to eat.

Lauren: These are the kids in our group.

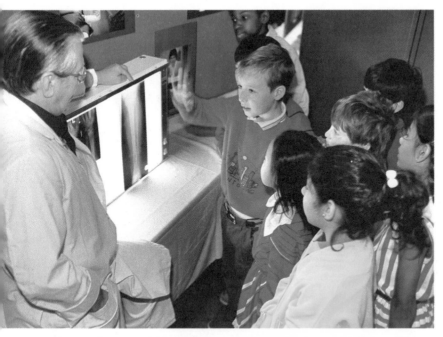

Lewis: The Cast Booth was our first stop at the Health Fair. The cast man showed us this **X-ray** picture of a broken bone. We could see the break if we looked closely.

Sui: I'm pretending to have a broken arm so the cast man can show us how he makes casts. First he wraps this soft bandage around my arm.

Next, he puts on another bandage full of wet plaster. It's all warm and squishy! When it dries, in about 48 hours, it will be almost as hard as a rock.

31

Maria: The nurses made little finger casts for all of us. I even learned how to make one myself.

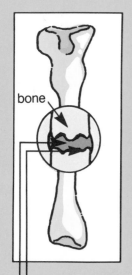
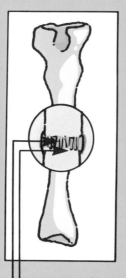
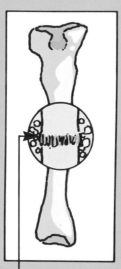
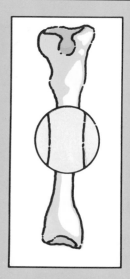

bone

- sharp end of broken bone
- blood clot

- ends get softer
- fibres grow through blood clot

- calcium helps new bone to form around break

new bone hardens and takes on normal shape

This diagram shows how a broken bone heals itself during the six weeks in a cast.

Richard: At the Eye Booth I tested my eyesight. I covered one eye at a time and read the vision chart. (That's the chart, behind me.) My vision is 20/20— normal.

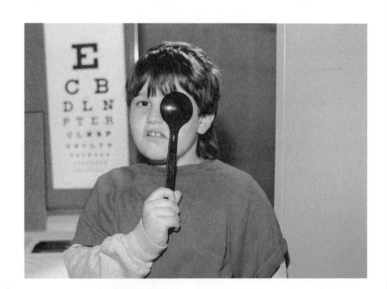

Lewis: Eye doctors use a flashlight and these special glasses to find out whether your eyes are straight.

The volunteer showed me diagrams of what happens to your pupil when light hits your eye.

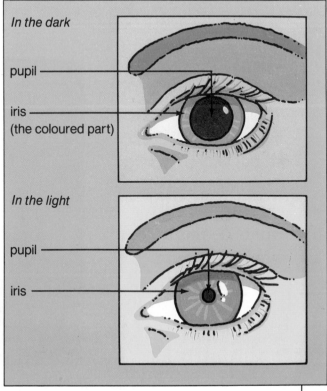

In the dark

pupil

iris
(the coloured part)

In the light

pupil

iris

Marianne: This is a big model of an ear. The part of your ear that you can see is the outer ear. But inside your head you have a middle ear and an inner ear, too.

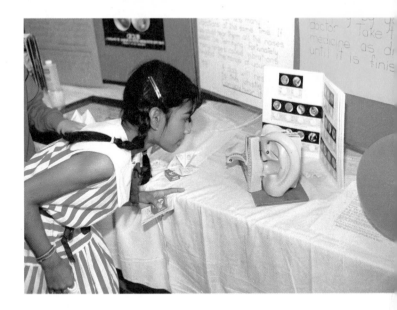

Lauren: I'm looking into Lewis's ear with an **auroscope**. It has a light in it, so I can see all the way to his ear drum. If Lewis had an earache, the doctor would do this to see what was wrong.

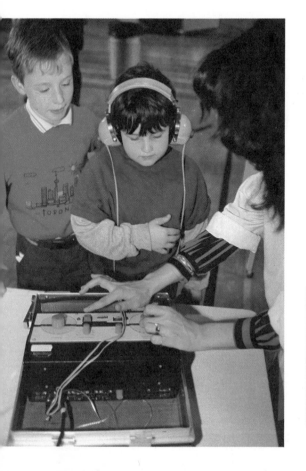

Richard: I'm listening to different sounds to compare how loud they are. The doctor said sounds are measured in **decibels (dB** for short). We saw a chart that showed different decibel levels.

You can imagine what 110 dB sounds like on headphones!

Whisper	- 30 dB
Talking	- 50 dB
Car	- 70 dB
Blender	- 90 dB
Motorcycle	- 110 dB

Maria: I'm listening while Amy talks into this hearing aid. It sounds fine if she uses her normal voice. But if she yells, the sound is too loud and fuzzy.

Amy: This is a bag of blood. I always thought it would look brighter red, like ketchup.

Robert: The Red Cross sent this blood to the Health Fair. Maybe it came from my parents. They gave blood to the Red Cross last week.

Maria: I asked why hospitals need blood. A nurse said they use it for people who lose a lot of blood in an accident or during an operation. The patient gets a blood **transfusion**.

Robert: I'm looking at some blood through this **microscope**. (It's an instrument that makes things look bigger.) I can see all kinds of funny little things swimming around.

They look like this.

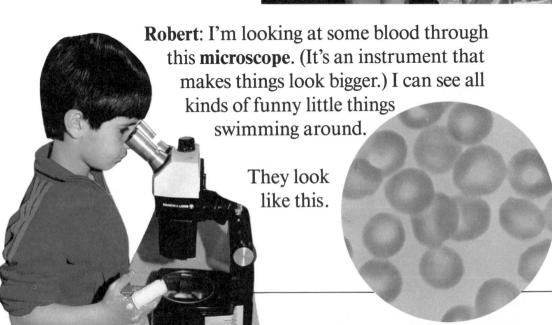

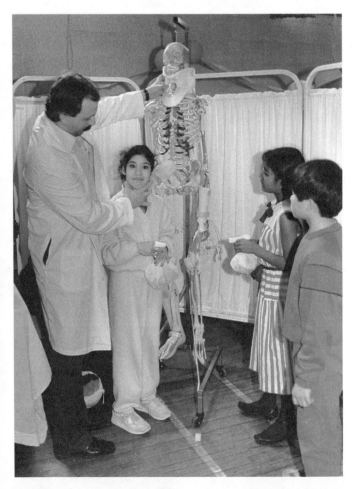

Maria: Professor Bones here is wearing a neck brace. He's probably been in a car accident. The doctor is showing me where he would put a neck brace on me.

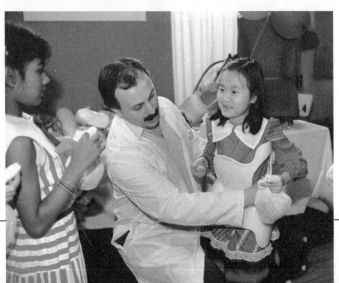

Amy: I'm being fitted with a body brace. Kids wear these if they need help keeping their spines straight. There are all kinds of braces—for arms, legs, feet, hips, necks, and back.

Maria: This machine measures your pulse— that's the number of times your heart beats in a minute. If you're 8 or 9 years old, your pulse should be about 70 beats per minute.

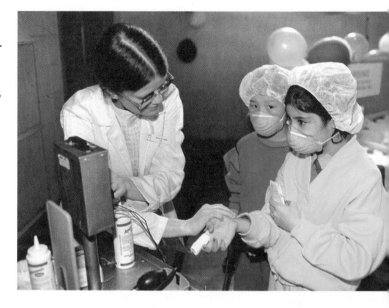

Marianne: How do you like my outfit? This is a surgical gown and it's what the doctors and nurses wear in the operating room. The medical cap keeps your hair out of the way. Everyone in the operating room wears a mask, too. It covers your nose and mouth so you don't spread germs to the patient.

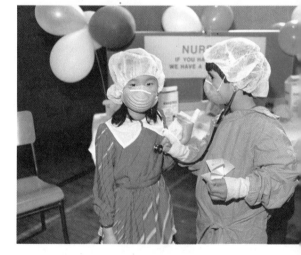

Robert: I listened to Amy's heartbeat using a **stethoscope**. It was neat. It sounded like lub-dub, lub-dub.

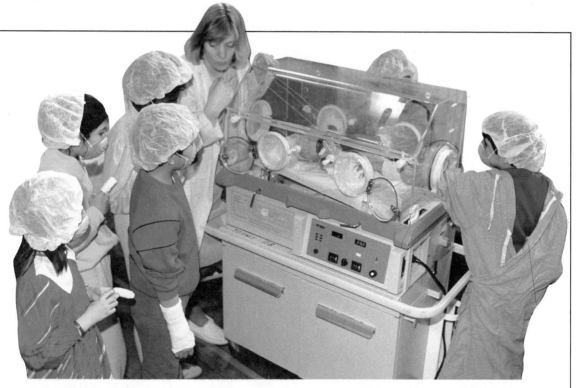

Marianne: This little plastic "bedroom" is called an **incubator**. It's warm and germ-free. Tiny babies who are sick or are born too soon stay in it until they are strong enough to go home with their parents.

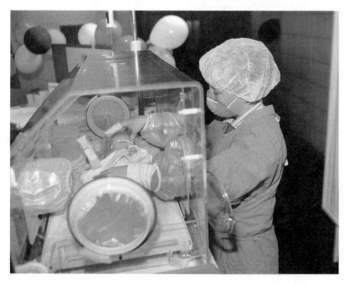

Lewis: There's a doll in this incubator. You can see the plastic "sleeves" around my arms. They stop germs from getting in and heat from getting out.

Sui: In this Nutrition Game we answered questions about good eating. Whenever we said the right answer, we got to take off another red square. The picture underneath was... Mr. T!

Lauren: This is the Poison Game. We had to put each bottle or can containing poisonous stuff in a place where little kids couldn't reach it.

Maria: This is OMNI the robot. He helps to cheer up the children who are sick and have to spend time in the hospital.

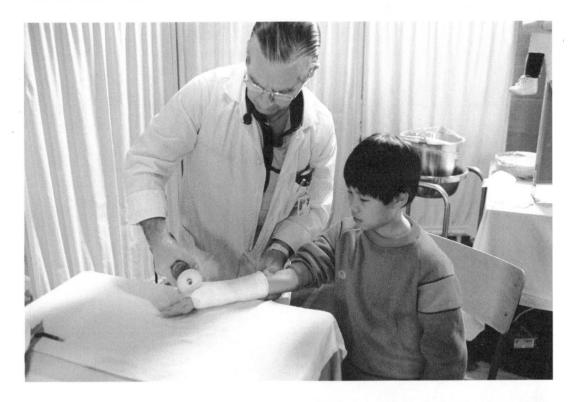

Sui: Before we went home, the cast man cut off my cast. You see that round saw of his? It cuts through the cast, but it doesn't cut skin. I didn't feel a thing! Everyone signed my cast, and I got to take it home.

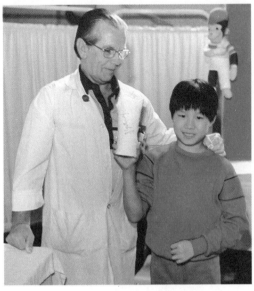

41

the trouble with stitches

by sean o huigin

the trouble
with having
stitches
is that it
really itches
as they heal
you get them
in all sorts
of ways
on rainy or
on sunny
days

by falling
or by getting
hit
so many ways
your skin
can split
and OW
OH WOW
you get them
on your arm or
head
they come from
falling out
of bed

on legs and
feet they're
sometimes
needed
anywhere you might
have bleeded
the doctor has
to put them in
with needles
not a safety pin
you often get
a bandage too
there is no
extra charge to you
for that
and then
you have to go
again
a week or two
or maybe three
later so the doc
can see
the bits of thread
and take them out
it doesn't hurt
no need to shout
they sometimes
go away themselves
perhaps that's
done by little
elves
at any rate
in any
weather
now your skin
will hold
together

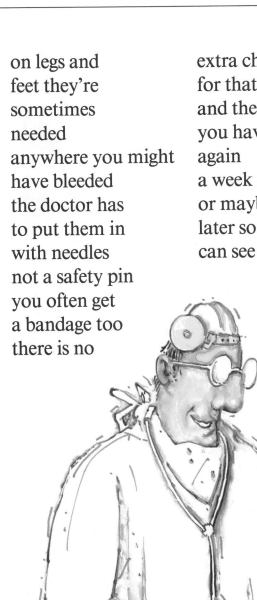

47

If Pigs Could Fly

...anything could happen!

It's So Nice to Have a Wolf Around the House

by Harry Allard

Once upon a time there was an old man who lived alone with his three old pets. There was his dog, Peppy, who was very old. There was his cat, Ginger, who was very, very old. And there was Lightning, his tropical fish, who was so old that she could barely swim and preferred to float.

One day the Old Man called his three pets together and said to them, "The trouble, my friends, is that we are all so very old." Peppy wagged his tail in agreement, but just barely; Ginger twitched her ears in agreement, but just barely; and Lightning waved her fin but fell over backward because of the effort involved.

"What we need," the Old Man continued, "is a charming companion—someone to take care of us and pep us up." Lightning and Ginger and Peppy thought the Old Man was right. But this time they were too tired to wag, twitch, or wave in agreement.

That very day the Old Man put an ad in the newspaper. The ad said: "Wanted: A charming companion. [Signed] The Old Man."

Early the next morning a furry stranger knocked on the Old Man's door. He had long white teeth and long black nails. Handing the old man an engraved visiting card, he introduced himself: "Cuthbert Q. Devine, at your service," he said, tipping his hat.

"Did you advertise for a charming companion, Old Man?"

"Yes, I did," the Old Man said.

"Look no further! I am the very one you have been searching for." Cuthbert smiled from ear to ear. "Many people think that I am a wolf. That, of course, is nonsense, utter nonsense. As a matter of fact, I happen to be a dog—a German shepherd to be exact." And Cuthbert laughed in a deep, wolfish voice.

The Old Man was completely dazzled by Cuthbert Q. Devine's charming personality. He particularly liked his big bright smile. And because the Old Man's eyesight was not what it used to be, he did not see Cuthbert for what he really was—a wolf!

"You are hired," the Old Man said. And Cuthbert Q. Devine moved in bag and baggage.

Cuthbert had not been on the job twenty-four hours before the Old Man and his three pets wondered how they had ever managed without him.

First up and last to bed, Cuthbert cleaned and cooked and paid the bills. He took Peppy for long walks, groomed Ginger, and fixed up Lightning's aquarium. He was a whiz at making fancy desserts.

He massaged the Old Man's toes. He played the viola. And every Saturday night he organized a fancy costume party.

If the Old Man had ever had any doubts about Cuthbert, they were all gone now. Cuthbert had a heart of gold. All he wanted to do was to make the Old Man and his three pets happy.

But it was all too good to last.

Late one afternoon, after Cuthbert had tucked him into his easy chair and handed him his paper, the Old Man read a terrible thing right on page one: "Wanted for Bank Robbery," the headline said. There was a picture of a wolf in a prison uniform. It was Cuthbert!

The Old Man could not believe his eyes.

"To think I hired him as a charming companion and he was a wolf the whole time!" The Old Man could not get over it. He was hurt. . .and frightened too.

Pale and shaking, the Old Man confronted Cuthbert in the kitchen. He waved the newspaper in Cuthbert's face. "And you told me you were a German shepherd," he said.

Cuthbert's spoon clattered to the kitchen floor.

"I'm no good," he sobbed. "No good at all. But I can't help it—I've never had a chance. I always wanted to be good, but everyone expected me to be bad because I'm a wolf."

And before the Old Man could say another word, Cuthbert fainted dead away.

Somehow Ginger and Peppy and the Old Man managed to drag Cuthbert to his bed. When the doctor arrived he said that Cuthbert had had a bad attack of nerves and would have to stay in bed for months if he was ever to get well again.

"You've got a very sick wolf on your hands," the doctor told the Old Man as he left.

Now it was the Old Man who got up early to clean and cook and pay the bills. But he did not mind at all—in fact he felt years younger. Peppy helped, so did Ginger.

With so much to do for Cuthbert, Peppy forgot his aches and pains; and everyone said that Ginger was as frisky as a kitten again.

Lightning did her share too: She spent her days blowing beautiful bubbles to amuse Cuthbert—it seemed to soothe his frayed nerves.

Cuthbert had to stay in bed for a long time, but at last he was well enough to get up. One day he told the Old Man how ashamed he was of robbing all those banks. He asked the Old Man what he should do.

On the Old Man's advice, Cuthbert turned himself in to the police. When his case came to court, Cuthbert promised the judge that he would never rob a bank again. The judge believed him and said, "I will let you go this time because you have done so much for the Old Man and his pets."

The Old Man was very happy. So was Cuthbert, but his paws shook from relief.

Cuthbert finally got completely well and lived with the Old Man and his three pets for the rest of their lives. As a matter of fact, all five of them are still living in Arizona to this day. The Old Man moved there with Lightning and Ginger and Peppy because the desert climate was better for Cuthbert's health.

The Mare

by Herbert Asquith

Look at the mare of Farmer Giles!
She's brushing her hooves on the mat;

Look at the mare of Farmer Giles!
She's knocked on the door, rat-a-tat!

With a clack of her hoof and a wave of her head
She's tucked herself up in the four-post bed,
　　　And she's wearing the Farmer's hat!

Nothing But a Pig

by Brock Cole

Once there was a poor man who had a pig he would not sell.

"It would be like selling a friend," he said to his wife. "Would you have me sell my friend?"

Of course his wife would not, and they managed as best they could on the money they earned selling fresh vegetables and eggs.

"They are not my friends," the poor man explained.

His name was Avril, his wife was Agnes, and his pig was named Preston.

In the evening after work Avril would go to the pigpen. There he would sit down and tell Preston about the events of his day. Preston was a good listener and enjoyed Avril's stories of village life.

But misunderstandings can occur between even the best of friends.

The truth is that Avril spoiled Preston. After a while, the pig began to think that he was finer than his poor friend.

"I was meant for better things," thought Preston.

"He thinks he is too good for the likes of me," thought Avril. "If he is not careful, I will sell him."

One day a rich man named Grabble, who owned the tiny cottage where Avril and Agnes lived, came to collect the yearly rent.

"The rent is doubled this year," said Mr. Grabble.

He had heard of Avril's fine pig, and wanted him for himself. He was very fond of bacon and ham.

"Then I cannot pay," said Avril.

"Then I shall have your pig," said Mr. Grabble.

"Well, why not?" thought Avril to himself. "He is, after all, nothing but a pig."

So he took Mr. Grabble to the pigpen.

When Preston saw the rich Mr. Grabble approaching, something stirred in his soul.

Mr. Grabble's shoes were shining. His suit fitted perfectly over his round stomach. His hair was combed neatly over the bald spot in the middle of his head, and he waved the flies away with a handkerchief that smelled of roses.

"Now there is a man I could admire," thought Preston.

"He'll do," said Mr. Grabble.

Mr. Grabble tied a rope to Preston's neck and led him away to his fine house in the village.

In the back of the Grabble house was a garden filled with flowers. At the end of the garden was a small pen, hidden by a bower of roses. There Mr. Grabble left Preston.

"What a fine house!" thought Preston. "What fine gardens!" He nibbled delicately at a spray of roses that hung over his pen.

Secretly he was disappointed that Mr. Grabble had not taken him into his house and introduced him to the family.

The truth struck him suddenly.

"I am not presentable! I need a bath, and"—he blushed pink with shame—"I have nothing to wear."

After a moment's thought, he unlatched the gate to his pen and walked to the back door of the house.

No one was in the kitchen. Preston refreshed himself with two cabbages and a bunch of carrots that had been left on the scrubbed table.

No one was in the hall... or on the stairs...or in the master bathroom.

Preston drew a bath and scrubbed himself thoroughly with Mr. Grabble's scented pink soap.

No one was in the dressing room where Mr. Grabble kept his fine clothes.

They fitted Preston admirably. In one of the pockets he found a pocket-book filled with money.

"How thoughtful of Mr. Grabble," said Preston to himself, "to see that I have everything that I need."

When the servant girl glanced into the parlour, she was startled.

"That must be Mr. Grabble's uncle, come to visit a day early, and no one to welcome him," she thought. She went into the parlour, curtsied low, and announced that Mr. Grabble had gone to his office at the bank, but that Mrs. Grabble would be back soon. She asked Preston if he would care for coffee and cake while he waited.

"Snort! Snuffle, gruff," said Preston politely.

"How gruff he is. I can barely understand him," thought the servant girl, "but his eyes are kind."

Away she went to fetch the coffee and cake.

At three o'clock Mrs. Grabble returned. She could hear someone playing the harmonium in the front parlour.

"It's Mr. Grabble's uncle, ma'am, come a day early," said the servant girl.

"Goodness!" said Mrs. Grabble, and went in to greet her husband's uncle.

"How stout he has grown," she thought.

"How well you look," she said.

She explained that they had not expected him so soon, and that Mr. Grabble had gone to the bank. Preston excused himself and went off to the bank to meet Mr. Grabble.

When he was gone, Mrs. Grabble went out into the garden to see the new pig. When she saw that the pig was gone and the gate was unlatched, she was very disturbed. She went back to the house to telephone her husband.

The servant girl met her at the door. She was very excited.

"A robber has taken Mr. Grabble's best suit, two cabbages, a bunch of carrots, and a bath," she said.

Mrs. Grabble said, "We must be calm. He has taken a pig as well. We can only be thankful that Mr. Grabble's uncle was not disturbed."

While the servant girl fixed her a cup of tea with four lumps of sugar, Mrs. Grabble telephoned her husband and told him what had happened. He was very annoyed. It made him feel only a little better to learn that his uncle had arrived a day early and was coming to his office to meet him.

In the meantime, Avril had begun to regret that he had given Preston to Mr. Grabble to be made into bacon and ham.

"My best friend," he said to his wife. "How could I have paid our rent with my best friend? I must have been insane."

He left for the bank immediately, determined to bring Preston back at any cost.

When he reached the bank and was shown into Mr. Grabble's office, he barely noticed the fine, portly gentleman standing by the window.

"Mr. Grabble," he began, "I made a terrible mistake this morning when I let you take my pig away. He is my best friend."

Preston (for, of course, Preston was the gentleman by the window) was deeply touched.

"Such devotion," he thought. "I had no idea."

Mr. Grabble, however, became angrier than ever. Since he no longer had Avril's pig, he decided to pretend that he had never had it.

"Pig? What pig? I don't have your dirty pig, and you owe me one year's rent," he shouted.

Preston was hurt and shocked by these words. "The man is a cad," he thought. He realized that he had been deceived by appearances.

Making up his mind instantly, Preston thrust his loaded purse into Avril's hands. The amount of money in the purse was exactly what Avril owed.

"Here is the rent," said Avril wonderingly.

"Sniffle, snort!" added Preston indignantly, and threw off Mr. Grabble's suit. He had learned that fine clothes do not make a man.

Avril was surprised that Preston was in the banker's office, but glad to have his friend back. Preston was sorry that he had considered leaving his friend even for a moment.

They went back to Avril's house together, where Agnes was waiting for them. That night they had a lovely supper of corn and turnips. It was delicious.

The Desert Is Alive

...and full of surprises.

DESERT WORLD

The rocks on the side of a river **canyon** have beautiful colours.

DESERT SCULPTURES

The desert is full of interesting shapes. In sandy deserts the wind blows the sand into hills called **sand dunes**. In rocky deserts, the wind wears away the rocks to form strange and beautiful sculptures.

The tall jagged rock is called a **butte**. The flat-topped hill is called a **mesa**.

Some deserts even have mountains with snow on top.

These sand dunes are shaped like the letter C.

These desert rocks are called **hoodoos**.

Some sand dunes are shaped like stars. Others look like rippling waves on a lake.

Badlands, Alberta

After a rain the **prickly pear cactus** comes into bloom. The cactus is juicy and watery inside. Its thorns keep away most of the thirsty animals, but the desert pack rat knows just where to nibble.

British Columbia

The **ponderosa pine** tree grows in dry valleys. Its roots grow deep into the dry earth to find water.

DESERT
PLANTS

Mexico

The **saguaro** is the biggest cactus. It grows very slowly but can live to be more than 100 years old.

Sahara Desert, Africa

The **date palm** tree will only grow in a place where there is lots of water all year round. An **oasis** is a place in the desert where there is a spring or a river to provide water.

From the air, a desert looks as if it has no life at all. But when you take a closer look, the desert begins to come alive. Let's look at some of the plants that live in deserts.

The **kit fox** hunts at night. Its large ears help it to hear the rustling sounds made by the rats it likes to eat.

The **chuckwalla lizard** escapes from its enemies by hiding in spaces between rocks. It gulps so much air that its body swells to fill the whole space. Not even its enemies can pull it out.

The **scorpion** has a poisonous stinger in its tail. It grasps insects in its claws, then kills them with its stinger. Baby scorpions ride on their mothers' backs for a week after they hatch.

DESERT ANIMALS

The **addax antelope** doesn't need to drink any water at all.

The **Arabian camel** can go for weeks without water, and even longer if there are plants to eat. Its toes are spread out wide to help it walk in the sand.

The **saw-scaled adder** is the most dangerous snake in the Sahara Desert. It makes a loud rasping sound like a saw. The adder glides across the sand in a sideways motion, leaving a double trail behind it.

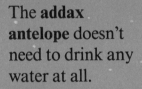

During the day, most of the animals that live in the desert hide to escape the heat. But at night, when it grows cool, they come out to hunt and to eat.

Desert sand is so hot that the **gerbil's** hind feet are covered in fur. Gerbils stay in their underground burrows until evening comes. They eat seeds, buds and insects.

75

The **gila woodpecker** pecks a hole in the giant saguaro cactus and builds its nest inside, to shield the eggs from the sun.

Elf owls often move into the nests the gila woodpeckers leave behind.

The **roadrunner** is a clumsy flyer, but a very fast runner. It is also a great snake catcher.

Another kind of owl, the **burrowing owl**, lives underground in the burrows that prairie dogs have abandoned.

DESERT BIRDS

AFRICA

Vultures are large birds that feed on animals which have died. Vultures have excellent vision. They fly high over the desert to spot dead animals. Then they flock down to eat.

AUSTRALIA

Millions of colourful **budgerigars** (budgies) live in the Outback— the desert area of Australia.

The **ostrich** grows as high as a classroom ceiling. It is too big to fly, but it is the fastest creature on two legs. It also lays the biggest eggs of any bird.

The desert is home for many different kinds of birds, large and small.

Sahara Desert, North Africa

The **Bedouin** people are **nomads**. They move about the desert on their camels, looking for pastures where they can feed their goats and sheep.

Egypt

Not all of the people who live in the Sahara Desert are nomads. Some people live in towns built beside an oasis. They grow vegetables and gather dates from the **date palm trees**.

DESERT
PEOPLE

Kalahari Desert, South Africa

The **Bushmen** who live here are also nomads, but they do not keep animals. Instead, they hunt wild animals and dig up roots and plants for food. Sometimes they store water underground in ostrich egg shells.

Southwest U.S.A.

This **pueblo** is hundreds of years old, and native people still live here. Thick walls and small windows protect the homes from the hot summer sun.

The desert is a home for people, too.

Lizard

by Byrd Baylor

When my mother laid her eggs
she looked for sand
that was just right.
It had to be damp
and it had to be warmed
all day by sun.

Down in that sand
she buried her eggs.

When she left,
she didn't come back.
There wasn't any need to.
Sand and sun
are mother enough
for lizards.

I dug my way
to sunlight.
It didn't take me long
to flick my tongue
and catch a gnat
and learn
that when the sun goes down
you can be warm
beneath a little mound
of sand.

It didn't take me long
to learn
the way
a lizard runs—
just a flash of speed
across the sand,
almost too fast
to be a shape.

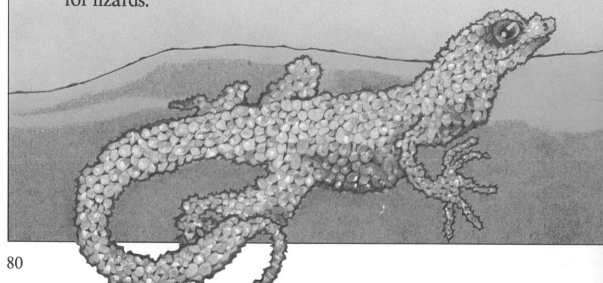

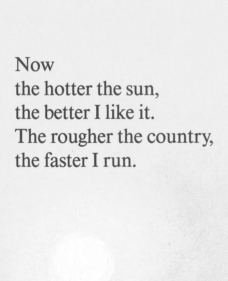

Now
the hotter the sun,
the better I like it.
The rougher the country,
the faster I run.

When I rest,
looking out over
the world
from a rock,
I show
the bright blue shining
colour of my underside.
I seem to be made
of earth
and sky.

But then
I run again
and I'm nothing
but a blur
in the hot white sun.

Cactus Wren
by Byrd Baylor

On the hottest
summer afternoons
when desert creatures
look for shade
and stay close to the earth
and keep their voices
low

I sit high on a cactus
and fling
my loud ringing trill
out to the sun...

over and over
again.

My home is
in a cholla cactus.
I won't live
where cactus doesn't grow
because I know
the only safe place
for a nest
is a stickery branch
in a cactus thicket.

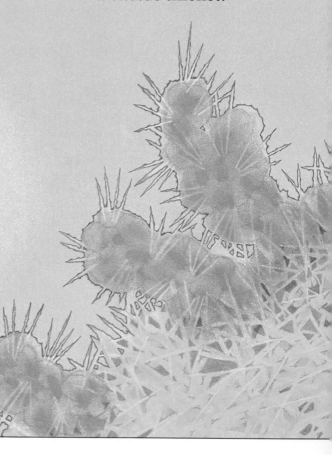

I like thorns
in all directions.

At the entrance
of my nest
I pile more cactus.
I peck off the spines
where I go
in and out.

It is so good a nest
that when we leave it
other creatures
will move in—
a family of crickets
or a cactus-climbing mouse.

But now
it holds
six small brown birds

and me.

You Can Call Me Badlands

by Lauren Wolk

My name's Betty Dawson, but you can call me
Badlands.

For my birthday last year, my parents gave me a
membership in the International Treasure Hunters'
Club. I got a really neat membership card and an
invitation to my first treasure hunt. The invitation said
that the hunt would begin at precisely 8:00 a.m. on
March 27 in Canada. I had to figure out exactly where.

I turned over the invitation and read the first clue
carefully. Here's what it said:

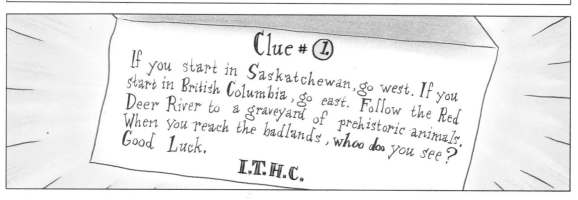

Clue # ①

If you start in Saskatchewan, go west. If you
start in British Columbia, go east. Follow the Red
Deer River to a graveyard of prehistoric animals.
When you reach the badlands, whoo doo you see?
Good Luck.

I.T.H.C.

Now, I come from a long line of treasure hunters. My grandmother started the famous Grandmothers-Who-Would-Rather-Hunt-For-Treasure-Than-Knit-Sweaters Club. My parents had to drop out of the Maritimes Treasure Hunt when I was born in their camper. And so, as soon as I read that clue, I felt my pulse begin to race. It was the treasure hunter in me, coming to the surface.

With some help from the library, my school atlas, and a few lucky guesses, I figured out where the hunt was going to begin.

It was 7:45 a.m. on March 27 when I joined several other people who were waiting for the park to open. I wondered if they were treasure hunters or just early risers, out for a jaunt through the park.

I also wondered about my second clue. Where would it be? "**Whoo doo** you see?" the first clue had said. I thought I'd figured out the weird spelling, but it wasn't until the park opened and I headed down into the badlands that I knew I was in the right place.

"Wow!" was all I could say as I wandered down into a canyon filled with wonderful, terrific, amazing hoodoos. It was like stumbling into a prehistoric world. "Whoo doo you see?" I asked myself, and suddenly the answer was right in front of me, staring me in the face. I waited until everyone else had moved on past me, and then I took a closer look.

It was a tiny hoodoo, just my size, and *this* hoodoo had a face. The wind and the rain had carved the soft sandstone into the spittin' image of Sir John A. Macdonald. I found the second clue tucked into his nostril. Here is what it said: ☞

Well, I followed the directions and nearly walked smack dab into a prickly pear cactus. "I 'get the point'," I muttered, and took a closer look.

There it was, the third clue, wedged between the sharp cactus spines. After trying to reach it with my finger, I opened my first bandaid, wrapped it around my wound, and tried a different approach.

Bubble gum worked like a charm. I chewed up a big wad until it was good and sticky, then I stuck a bit on the end of a twig and used it to grab the clue. Here's what this one said:

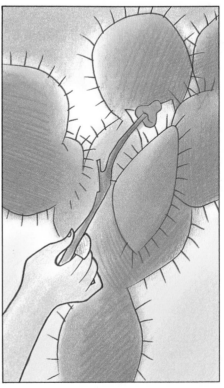

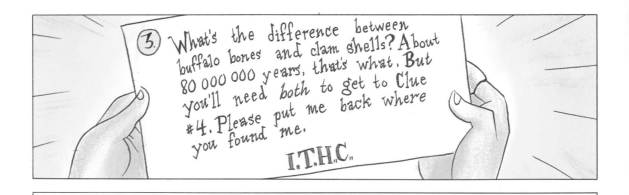

What's the difference between buffalo bones and clam shells? About 80 000 000 years, that's what. But you'll need both to get to Clue #4. Please put me back where you found me.

I.T.H.C.

The park map I'd brought along pointed out all kinds of neat stuff. Like, "Phred, a 250-year-old skeleton of a buffalo who got beaned with a falling rock." And, "80 000 000-year-old Mesozoic clam shells that will knock your socks off."

"Sounds like the stuff I'm looking for," I thought. So I went on a buffalo hunt and found Phred right where he'd been for the past 250 years. I looked around and saw something shiny on top of a tiny hoodoo.

"Find a penny, pick it up, and all the day you'll have good luck," I said as I stooped to get it. It turned out to be luckier than I thought. I'd found part of the fourth clue.

It was half of a small, copper disk, with a picture and a message engraved on it. It looked like this:

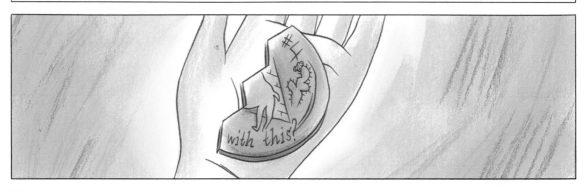

"Hmmmm," I thought. "I'm going to need the other half before I can figure out *this* clue." So I made a quick sketch of the half disk, put it back where I'd found it, and went to look for the Mesozoic clam shells of Dead Lodge Canyon.

When I found them, I spotted the second half of the disk perched on a clam fossil. When I placed it on the sketch I'd made of the first half, the clue looked like this:

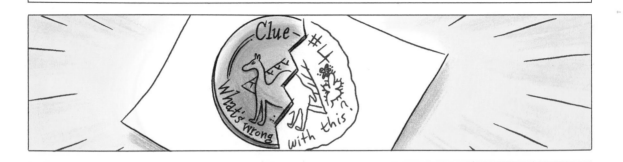

"What's wrong with this picture?" I asked myself. "Well, to begin with, this place isn't exactly crawling with camels." Then I remembered that I'd seen a picture of a camel not long before.

"Of course!" I cried, whipping open my park brochure to a photograph of the Valley of the Castles. It had some pretty amazing hoodoos and other formations—like a camel-lookalike and a pyramid, too. So, I finished my sketch of the copper disk, checked my map again, and went camel hunting.

The path I was following led me up, up, up along a steep canyon wall. Now, I'm not too crazy about heights. So when it suddenly began to get windy and dark, I went from being nervous to just plain scared.

I looked up and saw a great, thick mass of thunderheads settling over the canyon like a lid on a kettle. I threw myself flat on my face when lightning made a short, fierce stab at the highest hoodoo. And then it began to rain.

I thought I'd seen storms before, but this was something altogether new. The rain came down in one solid curtain of water. And, as I watched in horror, the badlands clay began to swell. I remembered that it was a special, extra-thirsty kind of clay, made from volcanic ash, and that it absorbed water like a sponge.

After about fifteen minutes, the rain suddenly stopped. So, naturally, I tried to stand up. That was when I found out how slippery wet badlands clay can be.

I zoomed back down the muddy path like a cannon ball, tumbling over and over, gathering speed as I went. At the bottom, I careened halfway across the rocky canyon floor before I finally came to a stop.

"Yeeeeeech!" I screamed, trying to spit the mud out of my mouth and wipe the goop out of my eyes. I must have looked like a monster to the poor kid I finally noticed standing a few metres away.

"Help!" I cried, but it sounded more like a wet sponge hitting a wall.

"Himalaya Harriet to the rescue!" she cried, and leaped into action. She wiped my eyes clean first, scraped most of the mud off my face, and then helped me rinse out my mouth and ears.

When I could finally talk again, I introduced myself and thanked her about a million times.

"What in the world were you doing?" she finally asked. "I mean, if you want to break some kind of world record, Niagara Falls in a barrel is a lot easier and a whole lot cleaner."

"It's a long story," I said, squeezing mud out of my hair. "I'm on a treasure hunt, you see, and I was on my way to the Valley of the Castles to find the camel formation when the storm broke."

"So *that's* what was on the disk," she said. "I found the first half, but I was just about to give up. The rain washed the second half away."

"*You're* a treasure hunter, too?" I asked.

"One of the best," she replied with a smile. "My specialty is mountains."

My specialty seemed to be mud, and I felt like a real beginner next to Himalaya Harriet. But I showed her my sketch of the disk, and the picture of the sandstone camel, and invited her to be my partner.

"I thought you'd never ask me," she said with a big grin, and we headed off down the canyon toward the Valley of the Castles.

When we got there, we carefully examined the camel and the pyramid. Nothing. Then we noticed the prickly pear. I looked at my sketch of the disk, and sure enough, the cactus was in the picture, too.

"That's funny," I said to Harriet. "Prickly pears don't have polka-dotted blossoms." But this one had a big, yellow bud with purple polka dots all over it. So I took a closer look: the flower was plastic! I peeled back the fake petals and found a tiny scroll where the pollen should have been.

"Eureka!" we cried, and read the scroll together. This is what it said:

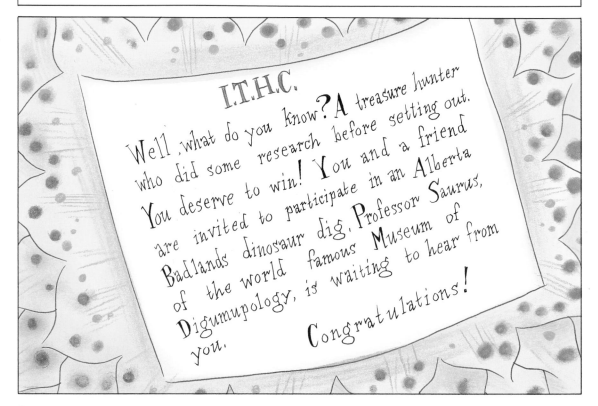

I.T.H.C.

Well, what do you know? A treasure hunter who did some research before setting out. You deserve to win! You and a friend are invited to participate in an Alberta Badlands dinosaur dig. Professor Saurus, of the world famous Museum of Digumupology, is waiting to hear from you. Congratulations!

"Congratulations, Betty!" Harriet said.

"Same to you, Harriet," I said. "The invitation is for both of us." While Harriet and I waited for the official I.T.H.C. helicopter to pick us up, she told me all about Sahara Sam, and Mississippi Martha, and all the other treasure hunters I hadn't met yet. And she told me about the hunt she'd won in Nepal—the one that gave her the name "Himalaya" Harriet. That's when I suddenly realized that I had a new name, too.

"Himalaya Harriet, meet Badlands Betty," I said proudly. "But you can call me Badlands." And the name stuck just like Badlands mud.

Project Manager: Jocelyn Van Huyse
Senior Editor: Sharon Jennings
Series Design: Rob McPhail and Lorraine Tuson
Design and Art Direction: Rob McPhail
Associate Designer: Glenn Mielke
Cover Illustration: Suzanne Duranceau
Typesetting: Trigraph Inc. ·
Printing: The Bryant Press Limited

Acknowledgements

Permission to reprint copyrighted material is gratefully acknowledged. Information that will enable the publisher to rectify error or omission will be welcomed.

Adaptation and abridgement of STEVIE by John Steptoe. Copyright © 1969 by John Steptoe. Reprinted by permission of Harper & Row, Publishers, Inc.

Shouting Doesn't Help. Used by permission of the author.

Maxie. Reprinted with permission of Four Winds Press, an Imprint of Macmillan Publishing Company from MAXIE by Mildred Kantrowitz. Text, Copyright © 1980 by Mildred Kantrowitz.

the trouble with stitches by sean o huigin. Reprinted by permission of Black Moss Press.

Text of NOTHING BUT A PIG by Brock Cole copyright © 1981 by Brock Cole. Reprinted by permission of Doubleday Company.

The Mare from PILLICOCK HILL by Herbert Asquith. Reprinted by permission of William Heinemann Limited.

Text and illustrations from IT'S SO NICE TO HAVE A WOLF AROUND THE HOUSE by Harry Allard. Copyright © 1977 by Harry Allard. Reprinted by permission of Doubleday & Company.

Byrd Baylor, *Cactus Wren* and *Lizard* from DESERT VOICES. Copyright © 1981 Byrd Baylor. Reprinted with the permission of Charles Scribner's Sons.

All other selections are used by permission of the authors.

Illustrations

Mark Craig: 5, 29, 49, 69; Susanna Denti: 14-19; VictoR GAD: 42-43; Don Gauthier: 44-48; Martine Gourbault: 59-68; Miro Malish: 58; James Marshall: 50-57; Glenn Mielke: 80-81, 82-83; Joe Morse: 20-28; Gordon Sauvé: 70-79; John Steptoe: 6-13; Maurice Vellekoop: 84-95; Tracy Walker: 32, 33, 35.

Photographs

Jeremy Jones: 30-41.

6 7 8 9 0 BP 3 2 1 0